The Snake
by the Lake

Mary Elizabeth Salzmann

Consulting Editor, Diane Craig, M.A./Reading Specialist

Published by ABDO Publishing Company, 4940 Viking Drive, Edina, Minnesota 55435.

Printed in the United States.

Credits
Edited by: Pam Price
Curriculum Coordinator: Nancy Tuminelly
Cover and Interior Design and Production: Mighty Media
Photo Credits: AbleStock, Brand X Pictures, Hemera, Photodisc, Wewerka Photography

Library of Congress Cataloging-in-Publication Data

Salzmann, Mary Elizabeth, 1968-
    The snake by the lake / Mary Elizabeth Salzmann.
        p. cm. -- (First rhymes)
    Includes index.
    ISBN 1-59679-529-8 (hardcover)
    ISBN 1-59679-530-1 (paperback)
        1. English language--Rhyme--Juvenile literature. I. Title. II. Series.
    PE1517.S3585 2005
    808.1--dc22

                                                                                    2005048803

SandCastle™ books are created by a professional team of educators, reading specialists, and content developers around five essential components that include phonemic awareness, phonics, vocabulary, text comprehension, and fluency. All books are written, reviewed, and leveled for guided reading and early intervention reading, and designed for use in shared, guided, and independent reading and writing activities to support a balanced approach to literacy instruction.

Let Us Know

After reading the book, SandCastle would like you to tell us your stories about reading. What is your favorite page? Was there something hard that you needed help with? Share the ups and downs of learning to read. We want to hear from you! To get posted on the ABDO Publishing Company Web site, send us e-mail at:

sandcastle@abdopub.com

SandCastle Level: Beginning

-ake

cake

lake

rake

shake

snake

Here is a .

Here is a  .

Here is a .

Here is a .

Here is a .

The cake is good.

The lake is wet.

The rake is long.

The shake is cold.

The snake is thin.

The Snake by the Lake

Jake has a cabin
by a little lake.

By the lake,
Jake likes to rake.

One day by the lake,
Jake got a snake
with the rake.

Jake likes the snake he got with the rake by the lake.

"I will bake it a cake!" says Jake.

By the lake,
Jake and the snake
he got with the rake
ate the cake
and a yummy shake!

About SandCastle™

A professional team of educators, reading specialists, and content developers created the SandCastle™ series to support young readers as they develop reading skills and strategies and increase their general knowledge. The SandCastle™ series has four levels that correspond to early literacy development in young children. The levels are provided to help teachers and parents select the appropriate books for young readers.

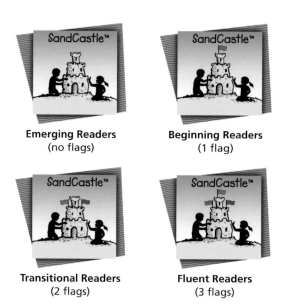

Emerging Readers
(no flags)

Beginning Readers
(1 flag)

Transitional Readers
(2 flags)

Fluent Readers
(3 flags)

These levels are meant only as a guide. All levels are subject to change.

To see a complete list of SandCastle™ books and other nonfiction titles from ABDO Publishing Company, visit **www.abdopub.com** or contact us at:
4940 Viking Drive, Edina, Minnesota 55435 • 1-800-800-1312 • fax: 1-952-831-1632